Thoughts That Became Poems

Ranaea Myers

Baptized

As I leaned back
I was sad
I was lost
I was broken
I was confused
I was angry
I just kept holding my breath
Feeling weighted and weightless at the same
time
I came up with a deep breath
Feeling happier and numb
Focused and aimless
too many emotions and indifferent
So am I worthy now?

Humble

The penalty for being self sufficient is being
classified as closed off
The penalty is being almost incapable of falling
for or dealing with mediocrity
I've been alone
I've been without intimacy
I've been without people blowing up my head
aside from virtually
Maybe when you get your heart broken things
fall into perspective
Maybe when you realize not even the strongest
love is exempt from disaster
You get humbled

Questions to ask yourself

If the love is not explosive
Why should I settle?
If the love is not explosive
Why should I risk being torn to pieces?
But how would I know If the love is explosive
Unless I reach out for it?

Selfish

If you want to be with me
I am going to unfairly require a lot of patience
and guidance.

Me?

What does it say about me
If I can have normal conversations
with anyone who has ever broke my heart?

From one God to another

I never could swim well but damn do I always
dive deep
Knowing I can't touch the bottom
Knowing I can't see what's beneath me
Knowing I can't let myself stay under
Is it crazy
Or is it brave
It's like staring down the barrel of a gun
Is it pride
Or is it because I just know what I'm doing
Or maybe I'm too scared to move
I'm somewhere between living in the fast lane
Reveling in love
Rebelling from it
Holding on to everything and nothing at all
Treading water in unfamiliar spaces
And drowning at the same time
That's my element though
Cool, calm, and, collected
Even in chaos
Panicking inwardly
But to you I'll move like a God with grace
It'll probably never change
It's just heavier than the water
I tread against

So just let me know when I can rest
Before this becomes second nature

Insatiable pt 2

I write
And I write and I write
Still I'm left empty
I want to throw all of these poems away
Delete them from existence
None of them measure up to the hole inside of
me
A permanent pit in my stomach
Staring out into the ocean with blank eyes
A chaotic mind
And a cold heart
Are my words not good enough because of the
words themselves
Or because I wrote them
Why do I continue to invalidate my own feelings
Only to turn around praising others

Give yourself more credit

The first time

Digging deep in you to find me
There's pain and beauty in having so many first
times' with a temporary person

If you love me

If you love me then show me
It is not an abstract concept

Found

I keep trying to find the most complete sentence
to describe how I feel or the exact word
Then I realized
Sometimes there's no description for being lost

Genetic

I always wondered if it was me
If I was the common denominator
If short comings were wired in my genes
If heartache and failure were genetic
I always wondered
As if there was no way I could ever suffice
because ruin was built in me

A poem you'll never read

I think I fell in love
Or something close to it
When I thought I couldn't love again
I told myself I'd never love again

I think I fell in love
With the way you talked to me
The way you dressed
The way you smelled

I think I fell in love with your ease
Your soul
The softness of your hands

The way we could laugh
I think I fell in love with how we vibed
like old friends

The way sound of your voice
The way I held you
The way you touched me

I think I fell in love with your words
Your music selection
The way you read your poetry

The way you knew a Maya Angelou poem upon
hearing it
I think I fell in love
Or maybe I just wanted to

Maybe you just woke me up
I spent years loving someone whose love had
dried up
I swear I fell in love

You're not mine to love
So I just have to admire you
Your secret admirer wondering if you admire me
too

So do you
Could you
Will you
Fall in love with me too

Or is that the easy way out
Because I fell into something
Knowing I had nothing to hold on to

Give yourself some too

Maybe that's the change I'd been waiting for
The rearrangement of my thoughts
The compassion for my own feelings
From me to me
How foolish I was to be extremely kind to others
While giving myself hell

Treat yourself better.

I'm proud of you

I lived
Yes
That is an accomplishment for me
Yes I'm proud of you

60 seconds

One minute I was everything
One minute I was the center of your world
I was cute
I was interesting
Do you remember

During that moment how I had your attention
We laughed
You smiled
You enjoyed my company
It had been the best minute I had experienced in
months

In that minute
I thought how there was no way someone could
be interested in me
Someone wanted to see me
Someone wanted to talk to me
Someone wanted to be around me

If it were up to me
I'd stay trapped in that minute forever
You were beautiful
Your tattoos were beautiful
Your skin was like honey

Your laugh
Your body
I couldn't believe it
There was no way
I wish I could have stayed in that minute
Because it's like once it passed
You refused to repeat it

I'm healing

You're never going to be a finished product
You're never going to be at your final form
There's not going to be a big signal that tells you
I'm ready for this
You just continue to work on yourself
Work on yourself
While allowing people to love you

Untitled

You want to understand me but I am not to be
understood
I'm neither here nor there
I am everywhere and nowhere at all

The sound of people with nothing

You had no home
While I was in mine
You sang as loud as you could
I wanted to tell you to stop
But I remembered that's all you had
That one song
On that cold night
That one song
On that cold night
Outside in your home

Final chapter of life with you

I think I was more inclined to write about you
Because I knew that here you and me would last
forever
But today
Today is the last day that I write about you
I let you go physically
Now the hard part.

All stars burn out

We met on an instant click
An instant explosion of you just get me
Pinging off of each other
A fire of "oh I like that"
"That's crazy, me too"
We drank wine, dined, laughed
while bonding over lost love
It takes oxygen to fuel a fire
My oh my did you breathe on it
You had problems
I had problems
No aliment outweighed the other
I knew there was a catch
One I said I accepted in an undertone
I knew it was too good to be true
Dammit do I always want it to be true
I knew I was on borrowed time by day two
But I couldn't help but be swallowed by you
I couldn't help but vibe with you
Speak with my patented charm to you
I observed as you did things only someone who
cared would do
Immediately after you finished
I watched you turn to ash right where you stood
Imprinted right where you would lay

I didn't understand your game
Why would you hold me like that?
Why would you touch me like that?
Why dig deep in my mind like that?
Why interlock yourself with me?
Why kiss my forehead like that?
Making all of your time align with mine
Then fading in and out
Mixing up different acts to throw at me
It's like you existed to show me something
I'm no fool I knew who you were
You're a professional
I knew it was a game
In an alternate universe maybe I'm your equal
I wonder if I made an impression on you
The same way I allowed you to make one on me
Or rather
How I allowed myself to believe that you made
one on me
I can't deny I wanted to try it
To charm my way into your life
But no I didn't even try it
I was only myself
That's how I sleep at night knowing that I was
myself
Knowing you had reservations
Knowing that "we" weren't meant to be
Knowing it would be a flame that died slow and
burned fast

You knew the end before you closed the curtains
You played us in reverse
But this is only my version of events

If I'm worthy enough to be etched in your pages
I'll see it from your view.

Euphoria

"Because I'm in love with you" she said

You're in love with me
You would climb to heights for me
Plunge into depths for me

You're in love with me
You're feeling an emotion
I no longer associate with

Love use to make my heart swoon
It use to take me to heights only addicts could
dream of

It's just
I know that you love me now
So I wonder when you'll stop
Those who have loved me have all but
disappeared

Being me has never given me a free pass
Hearing that you love me would mean
I'm one step closing to you leaving

I'm one step closer to falling in love alone

Your revelation begins the countdown
Slowly ticking until you've had enough

Until you find that thing about me
That one thing that's too much

Until I make that mistake that's unforgivable
I know you love me now
But every now is followed by then

So when
not if
When you stop loving me I won't be upset

I've learned ways to lessen the strike
I brace myself for the blow
You're in love with me
There's no doubt that you mean it

You're in love with me
I love you too
Not if but when you stop loving me

I know you'll mean that too

www.ingramcontent.com/pod-product-compliance
Lightning Source LLC
Chambersburg PA
CBHW070733160726
48003CB00006BA/2489